Scrum

The Complete Step-By-Step Guide to Managing Product Development Using Agile Framework

Jeffrey Ries

© **Copyright 2018 by Jeffrey Ries. All rights reserved.**

This document is geared towards providing exact and reliable information regarding topic and issue covered. The publication is sold with the idea that the publisher is not required to render accounting, officially permitted, or otherwise, qualified services. If advice is necessary, legal or professional, a practiced individual in the profession should be ordered.

From a Declaration of Principles which was accepted and approved equally by a Committee of the American Bar Association and a Committee of Publishers and Associations.
In no way is it legal to reproduce, duplicate, or transmit any part of this document in either electronic means or in printed format. Recording of this publication is strictly prohibited and any storage of this document is not allowed unless with written permission from the publisher. All rights reserved.

The information provided herein is stated to be truthful and consistent, in that any liability, in terms of inattention or otherwise, by any usage or abuse of any policies, processes, or directions contained within is the solitary and utter responsibility of the recipient reader. Under no circumstances will any legal responsibility or blame be held against the publisher for any reparation, damages, or monetary loss due to the information herein, either directly or indirectly.

Respective authors own all copyrights not held by the publisher.
The information herein is offered for informational purposes solely, and is universal as so. The presentation of the information is without contract or any type of guarantee assurance.

The trademarks that are used are without any consent, and the publication of the trademark is without permission or backing by the trademark owner. All trademarks and brands within this book are for clarifying purposes only and are the owned by the owners themselves, not affiliated with this document.

Table of Contents

Introduction 4

Chapter 1: Basics of Scrum 6

Chapter 2: The Sprint 15

Chapter 3: Looking Back on a Sprint and Planning for the Future 25

Chapter 4: Artifacts of Scrum 29

Chapter 5: Scrum Master as Servant Leader 34

Chapter 6: Making the Scrum Transition 44

Chapter 7: Tips for Success 49

Chapter 8: Stories from the Trenches 59

Conclusion 64

Introduction

Congratulations on getting a copy of *Scrum: The Complete Step-By-Step Guide to Managing Product Development Using Agile Framework* and thank you for doing so.

When it comes to improving your team's ability to generate useful iterations of a product in a reasonable amount of time, while at the same time ensuring they have the tools they need to cut out as much waste as possible, there is no better choice than a Scrum framework.

While it may have developed a reputation over the years for being somewhat obtuse, this is only because its approach is so much different than what the average team expects that it can seem arcane without a little guidance. As such, this book is here to guide you through the ins and outs of the Scrum process to ensure your team gets on the road to improved efficiency as soon as possible.

First, you will learn all about the basics of Scrum including its underlying philosophy and what makes it so effective. Next, you will learn about the main event in the Scrum process, the Sprint, why it matters and how it will help improve efficiency across the board.

From there, you will also learn about the key artifacts in Scrum and the Scrum Master and how they all work together to improve efficiency on all sides. From there, you will learn about the practical side of the process including how to make the transition to Scrum as well as tips for success while doing so. Finally, you will learn about the success stories of companies from all around the world that have made the transition and seen great results because of it.

There are plenty of books on this subject on the market, thanks again for choosing this one! Every effort was made to ensure it is full of as much useful information as possible, please enjoy!

Chapter 1: Basics of Scrum

Scrum is a process framework in which team members can deal with a wide variety of complex and ever-changing problems in a creative fashion while at the same time remaining productive and delivering products that meet or exceed expectations. While Scrum is relatively lightweight and easy to understand at a basic level, it can also be extremely complex and take years to master.

It was created in the early 1990s by Jeff Sutherland and Ken Schwaber for use in software development but has since been used in a wide variety of other industries as well. Scrum's greatest strength is that it makes it very easy to determine the overall efficacy of work techniques and product management while also making it easier to deal with the issues that come along with striving to continuously improvement the working environment, team and product.

The Scrum framework is made up of various Scrum Teams as well as their associated rules, artifacts, events and roles. Each of these components then serves a very specific purpose, with the whole coming together to be essential to the Scrum framework's continued usage and overall success. Meanwhile, the rules of Scrum are what bind the interactions between the main relationships, artifacts, events and roles that make the Scrum framework work as effectively as possible.

Scrum uses

While Scrum was initially used to develop products, for nearly 30 years it has been used in a wide variety of industries to do things like:

- Determine viable markets, products and technologies
- Identify products ripe for refinement or enhancement
- Iterating and producing new versions of products or additions as quickly as possible
- Sustain existing operational environments and create new ones including cloud environments
- Renew and sustain existing products

Due to its rapid iteration process, Scrum has been used extensively when it comes to developing hardware, software, embedded software and the like. It has also been used for almost everything else including autonomous vehicle creation, governments, schools, marketing strategies and organizational operations too numerous to mention.

While it was created nearly 30 years ago, as the interactions between environmental, market and technological complexities have grown, Scrum has proved its utility when it comes to dealing with life's complexities on a near daily basis. It has also proven especially adept at improving processes related to incremental and iterative transfers of knowledge.

At its heart, Scrum is all about small teams of people working together as effectively as possible. These teams are extremely adaptive and flexible and these strengths can be maintained regardless of how many teams are concurrently working side by side. These teams are then able to interoperate and collaborate via a mixture of targeted developmental architectures and sophisticated release environments. When discussing Scrum, the words development and develop are used when referring to any type of complex work that may be taking place.

Basics of Scrum Theory

The basics of Scrum can be found in the empirical process control theory which itself is part of the philosophy of empiricism. The basic idea behind empiricism is that knowledge is gained most effectively via experience and making the best possible decision at the moment with the information that is available. To take advantage of this idea, Scrum uses an incremental an iterative approach as a means of control risk and increasing the predictability of the desired outcome. There are three pillars at play when the empirical process is used, adaptation, inspection and transparency.

Transparency: Transparency is vital as it is important that those who are responsible for the outcome of a given process have a clear understanding of how it is proceeding at every step along the way. Additionally, transparency is also important to ensure that anyone else who needs to see what is going on can follow along as well. The end goal is that any observers will all have the same general understanding of whatever it is they are seeing.

One such area in which this is the case is when it comes to having a common language throughout the process that can be shared by everyone who has a hand in it. For example, those creating the product and those looking at the results will both need to have the same understanding of when the project is actually completed.

Inspection: Scrum users are frequently required to use Scrum artifacts as they progress towards a goal in order to determine potential variances that may be undesirable to that goal. These inspections should not be so frequent that the get in the way of the work that is being completed and are instead most effective when they are performed diligently by those who are skilled at inspecting this point of work.

Adaptation: When an inspector finds that some aspect or aspects of the process are deviating more than is acceptable, or that the resulting product will ultimately be unacceptable then the process must be changed as quickly as can be managed to avoid additional deviation as much as possible. When adaptation is required, there are several specific events that take place as part of the Scrum process and they include the Sprint Retrospective, Daily Scrum, Sprint Review and Sprint Planning.

To ensure the pillars of Scrum all work at maximum efficiency while at the same time building trust among the group as a whole, the entire Scrum team needs to live by the values of respect, openness, focus, courage and commitment. Scrum team members explore and learn to embody these values as they work with various Scrum artifacts, roles and events. Using Scrum successfully ultimately requires team members to become more adapt at living these specific values over time. Likewise, it is important that the team feel the need to personally commit to achieving the goals of the Scrum team as well.

It is important that the Scrum team feels supported enough to have the courage to always do the right thing on a project, regardless of how difficult it might seem at the time. If the Scrum Team and its various types of stakeholders can all ultimately agree to be open about the work that is being done and the challenges being faced then mutual respect will flourish and everyone can focus on the work of each Sprint and the ultimate goals of the team.

Members of the team

The Scrum team is made up of the Scrum Master, Development Team and the Product Owner. Scrum teams tend to be both cross-functional and self-organizing which means the member of the team will be responsible for choosing how to accomplish their work most effectively as opposed to being directed one place or another by one person or, even worse, someone outside the team entirely. A team is considered cross-functional, however, if it consists of multiple people who can accomplish each part of the goal thus making it possible to virtually ensure the team never has to rely on anyone else to get the job done. The Scrum team model was designed to optimize flexibility, productivity and creativity.

The Scrum team works on an iterative basis which means they deliver products incrementally with the goal of ensuring there are as many opportunities to receive feedback as possible. Each new version is as complete as possible so, at the very least, a version of the project that is usable to some degree is always readily available.

Product owner: The Product Owner is the member of the team who is in charge of ensuring the work of the Development Team is used to its maximum efficiency. What this means is going to vary dramatically based on the industry of the project as well as the individual Product Owner. One thing that will never change, however, is that the Product Owner is the only person who is responsible for managing any product backlog. These tasks can be given to the Development Team but the Product Owner will remain accountable for them. These tasks include things like:

- Expressing available items in the Product Backlog in a clear and concise manner
- Placing these items in order to ensure they are aligned in such a way that best achieves missions and goals
- Work to ensure the backlog is clearly visible to everyone so the next task to be worked on is clear

It is important that the Product Owner is always a single person rather than a group of individuals, though they may work towards the goals of a group if they prefer. Regardless, if the priority of a given item is going to change, the Product Owner needs to give the okay. In order for the Product Owner to ultimately succeed at their task, it is important that it is made clear the entire organization respects their decisions. Likewise, it must be clear that no one else has the power to change what the Development Team is working on or what their current requirements are.

Development Team: The Development Team is made up of those who actually do the work when it comes to creating something that can be labeled as "Done". This is naturally the end of the current Sprint as it is required to move onto the Sprint Review portion of the process. Only the members of this team are allowed to create the Increment.

The Development Team should be structured in such a way that its members feel empowered to do things like managing their own work and organize as they see fit. The resulting synergy this creates serves to optimize their overall effectiveness and efficiency. Good development teams have the following characteristics:

- They have the autonomy to take Backlog items and turn them into Increments that are potentially useable as they deem fit
- Development Team members are Development Team members, there is no further designation in the space
- Likewise, there are no official sub-teams within the Development Team, they can congregate at will
- All accountability is shared throughout the entire team

The size of the Development Team should be small enough that it can pivot as needed, while still being large enough to complete a reasonable amount of work within each Sprint. Generally speaking, if your Development Team doesn't contain at least three individuals then you will tend to see less interaction overall and thus smaller gains when it comes to productivity. Likewise, smaller teams are more likely to be constrained by the skills they do or do not possess, eventually getting to a point where they can't actively improve the Increment in question without going outside the team.

On the other hand, anything more than 10 people can make it difficult to coordinate everyone effectively, leading to decreased gains as well. Additionally, they can add so many moving pieces to the puzzle that the empirical process begins to break down. The Scrum Master and the Product Owner are not included in this classification unless they are actively working on the Sprint Backlog as well.

Chapter 2: The Sprint

While the organizational style of Scrum is relatively freeform, it still uses numerous events to help add some regularity to the process and also to minimize the need for extraneous events that are not directly prescribed by Scrum. Any Scrum events are going to be time-boxed by nature which means that each will have a maximum possible duration. The Sprint is the primary event in the Scrum process in that it contains all the other events that may take place during the creation of one iteration of a product. After a sprint has started its duration is set in stone and cannot be changed regardless if it is to lengthen or shorten it.

The events within the Sprint can all be seen as a separate opportunity to either adapt or inspect something. These events are especially designed to enable the level of detailed inspection that allows for true transparency when it comes to critical processes. As such, if any of these events are missed or skipped for any reason the end result is a weakened ability for the Scrum team to inspect the process and adapt it accordingly, leading to an overall reduced level of transparency that will hurt not only the current Sprint but all additional Sprints moving forward that are based on the incomplete data.

The Sprint

The Sprint is a time-box that lasts no more than a month during which the Scrum team will generate a completed product that is potentially releasable but certainly useable in some capacity which is referred to internally as an Increment. Sprints should each have the same duration throughout the development of the product in question. A new Sprint should start as soon as the last one ends. Each Sprint will consist of various segments including Sprint Planning, Development Work, Daily Scrums and the Sprint Retrospective.

During each Sprint, it is vital that there are no changes made to the scope of the product or Increment that would make it impossible to reach the current Sprint Goal. Likewise, quality goals cannot decrease during the Sprint, though the scope can potentially be renegotiated or clarified if the Product Owner and the Development Team decide that earlier projections were incorrect.

Each Sprint can be considered a type of project with a horizon of a maximum of one month. Like projects, Sprints are used to accomplish something specific which means that each Sprint will naturally have a goal when it comes to what is going to be built, what the design is going to be like and a general, flexible, plan that will set the Development Team on the right track. It will also have a clearly defined scope of the work to be done and what the resulting increment will be.

It is important to ensure that the scope of the Sprint doesn't end up growing so long that you are tempted to expand its length. If the horizon for a specific Sprint grows too long, the scope is likely to change too much and the overall complexity and risk may change it into something else entirely. Sprints are useful because they are predictable and they are predictable because it is possible to ensure adaptation and inspection but most importantly progress towards the goal in a reasonable amount of time. Keeping the Sprint length limited also keeps costs easier to track on a monthly basis.

Sprint cancellation: While a Sprint can't be extended, there is a possibility that it could be cancelled before the Sprint timebox is naturally finished. However, the only person who has the authority to do so is the Product Owner, though they may listen to anyone else involved in the matter, including the shareholders as well as the Scrum Master and the Development Team.

Generally speaking, the only real reason to cancel a Sprint once it is up and running is if the Sprint Goal becomes obsolete. This might happen if the company changes its goals while the Sprint is in progress, or if the technology conditions or market change overall. Generally speaking, however, a Sprint should only if it no longer makes any sense given the current circumstances. This should rarely occur due to the short amount of time that a Sprint is active for, however, especially as the timeframe is quite short.

If a Sprint is canceled, then the first thing that should happen is that any product backlog items that have been generated are reviewed. If any of the Increments are useable or releasable then the Product Owner will accept it while the incomplete items are returned to the backlog with a new estimate towards their completion. Any work that is not immediately useable often has a short shelf-life and will need to be re-estimated if it will ever be used properly.

It is important to keep in mind that if a Sprint is canceled then all of its consumed resources are lost because of what is not reusable. What's more, additional resources are going to be required before anything useful is generated as the Scrum team needs to go back to square one in order to get back to work. As such, the cancellation of a Sprint is often seen as quite traumatic to a team and should be avoided if at all possible.

Planning the Sprint: Any work that is going to be generated during the Sprint should first be discussed during the Sprint Planning portion of Sprint. This plan should be created in a collaborative fashion and include the entirety of the Scrum team. Sprint Planning should be kept to less than eight hours each month, with shorter Sprints having shorter planning periods as well. The Scrum Master is in charge of ensuring that all of the events take place on time and that everyone in attendants is on the same page regarding desired results. The Scrum Master should also be the one in charge of keeping everyone else working within the predetermined time-box.

A quality session of Sprint Planning should answer several questions starting with providing a clear estimation of what can be delivered from the Increment that the Sprint will be creating and how the work that is required be completed. The Development Team is in charge of deciding what types of functionality will be integrated into the next Increment for the upcoming Sprint. Meanwhile, it is the job of the Product Owner to discuss the purpose of the current Sprint Goal and note the items in the backlog that they believe would help to reach it and would, thus, be most effective in helping everyone achieve their goals. Meanwhile, the entirety of the Scrum team should collaborate in the understanding of the work the Sprint is doing.

The real input for this meeting should include the past project history for the Development Team, their capacity, the most recent increment of the product and the available product backlog. The number of items chosen from the backlog for this Sprint is going to be up to the Development Team as they are the only ones that can accurately determine what they are going to accomplish during the Sprint.

During this period is also when the Scrum team as a whole creates the goal for the next Sprint. This goal should be the main objective that will be met during the Sprint based on the items chosen from the backlog and should serve to guide the Development team throughout the process of building the next increment.

When it comes to determining exactly how the work in question is going to be completed, the Development team determines this aspect of the process after the Sprint Goal has been created and the next round of backlog items has been chosen. The Development team has complete control when it comes to determining how best to add the chosen functionality to the next Increment. This work will naturally require varying levels of effort and work from smaller groups within the Development team of various sizes.

While this outline doesn't need to be exactingly precise, it does need to be formalized enough to determine the scope of what can be completed during the next Sprint. Additionally, this meeting should break down exactly what needs to be done for the early days of the Sprint, generally broken into units of a single day. This plan should then be presented to the Product Owner who may be needed to help clarify specifics regarding backlog items and offer up trade-offs that can be made if the Development Team has too little or too much to do for the next Sprint. Other team member or stakeholders may be invited to this portion of the meeting with the Development Team go-ahead as well.

By the end of the planning portion of the Sprint, the Development Team should be able to concisely explain how the work will be completed during the Sprint to reach the target goals in questions. If there is any uncertainty regarding this fact then this is where it will be hashed out as after this the Sprint shifts into high gear.

Sprint Goal: The guiding principal behind the Sprint Goal is that it provides clear guidance to the Development Team when it comes to creating the best increment possible. A good Sprint goal is one that provides the Development team with a fair amount of flexibility when it comes to the functionality that is ultimately created during the Sprint. Any backlog items that are chosen should all work to deliver on a single element of the products function, which is often reflected in the goal for the specific Sprint as well. It can also be any other type of coherence that serves to keep the Development Team working together towards a common goal as opposed to splintering into numerous smaller, more personal, goals.

While the Development Team is in the midst of a Sprint, it should also keep the Sprint Goal and what is required in order to see it completed successfully in mind. If during the Sprint, the work takes an unexpected turn it is then the responsibility of the Development Team to speak to the Product Owner to ensure that the Sprint can proceed successfully.

Daily Scrum: The Daily Scrum is a 15-minute event that should have its own time-box during which the Development Team can discuss what they will be working on between now and the next Daily Scrum. This will make it possible to optimize the team as effectively as possible for the work that is to come, while also providing a clear path for everyone to follow to keep everyone working towards the same vision. The Daily Scrum should be held at the exact same time every day if at all possible to allow it to be the cornerstone of the Development Team's workday.

Daily Scrums are vital when it comes to ensuring open communication between the Development Team, often to the point that they remove the need for other meetings entirely, thus naturally increasing productivity as a result. They also make it possible for the entire team to be aware of any impediments to the Sprint as quickly as possible. Their daily nature also ensures the team has the ability to make decisions quickly while improving their knowledge at the same time. As such, it is a key component when it comes to the Sprint's ability to improve thanks to adaptation and inspection.

The Development Team should use the Daily Scrum as an opportunity to inspect the progress that has been made towards the Sprint Goal already and what is going to be done next as well. The Daily Scrum is exceedingly useful as it gives the entire team a place to discuss issues that might make it difficult for the Sprint to be completed on schedule. With the whole team aware of the problem, solving it becomes far more manageable, and will take much less time than would otherwise be the case. It also gives the team an opportunity to reorganize as needed to ensure peak efficiency is ensured and reconfirmed each and every day.

The structure of this meeting should be as fluid as the Development Team itself, and the most important thing is that the end result is effective for those who are using it. Some Development Teams start off each meeting with a list of questions to be answered about the current and future state of the Increment while others are more discussion based. Again, the format that your Development Team chooses isn't nearly as important as the fact that it works for them.

The job of the Scrum Master, in this instance, is to ensure that the Development Team holds their meeting, while at the same time not trying to direct the Daily Scrum itself. It is also the Scrum Master's job to ensure the Daily Scrum doesn't exceed its designated time box. Finally, as this is an internal meeting for the Development Team, the Scrum Master should also work to ensure that other team members don't disrupt the meeting.

Chapter 3: Looking Back on a Sprint and Planning for the Future

Sprint review: The Sprint Review is held at the conclusion of each Sprint as a means for the entire Scrum Team and any relevant stakeholders to take a look at the new Increment together for the purposes of determining what changes, if any, need to be made to the new Product Backlog. Throughout the Sprint Review process, the team should discuss how the entire Sprint proceeded, and what can be done to further optimize value in the future.

Nevertheless, this is not a status meeting, it is more informal than that with the presentation of the Increment serving as a means of fostering collaboration and eliciting quality feedback. Assuming the Sprint lasted a full month, the meeting should be no longer than four hours. The Scrum Master is the one in charge of ensuring that this event takes place and that everyone involves correctly understands its purpose. They should also be in charge of keeping the meeting to a reasonable length in proportion to the length of the Sprint.

Every Sprint Review needs to include numerous elements, starting with the attendance; the review should include the

Scrum Master, the Product Owner, the Development Team and any stakeholders the Product Owner deems fit. The review should then start with the Product Owner discussing what items have been checked off the product backlog with this iteration and what still needs to be completed before everything is said and done.

From there, the Development Team should discuss everything that went well throughout the Sprint as well as the problems that they face and how they overcome them. They will also demonstrate anything new that the iteration can do as a result of the Sprint and answer any questions from the wider team about this specific Increment.

The Product Owner should then discuss the current state of the product backlog as well as the new delivery date for the final, final product based on the current progress. From there, the entire group should collaborate on what to do next so that the Sprint Review provides useful input for the next round of planning. This should also include a general review of the way in which the marketplace or target audience for the product might have changed during the last Sprint and if anything else needs to change as a response.

Finally, the entire team should review the new details surrounding the product as a whole as well as the current

Increment and what the next Increment will look like assuming everything goes according to plan. Anything new is then added to the product backlog as needed.

Sprint retrospective: The Sprint Retrospective is the last opportunity for the team to check in with one another and ensure that there is a plan for enacting any changes that need to take place prior to the start of the next Sprint. Assuming your Sprint lasted one month, this meeting should last no longer than three hours. The Scrum Master should be in charge of keeping everyone on task for the meeting as well as ensuring that it stays within a reasonable timeframe. At the same time, however, the Scrum Master needs to participate as a peer in this meeting as well to ensure they feel the right level of accountability for the Scrum process as a whole.

The goal of the Sprint Retrospective is for the team to understand how effective the last Sprint was in regard to the tools used, processes streamlined, relationships formed and the people involved. This should include a look at what went well and what went poorly as well to ensure that when the team creates a plan for improvement with the next Sprint it accurately covers the scope of what needs to be done.

During this time the Scrum Master should do what they can to ensure the Scrum Team improves, while at the same time keeping everyone tied to the Scrum process framework with the end goal of making the process not only effective but also as enjoyable as work can be. For each Retrospective, the team should emerge with new ways of increasing product quality through an improvement to work process and possibly a change in what the definition of finished for the next Sprint will be. Assuming, of course, these changes don't create a conflict between organizational or product standards.

By the end of each Retrospective, the entire team should have a clear idea of the improvements that will be implemented for the upcoming Sprint. Ensuring these improvements are implemented is where the adaptation part of the process comes into play. While various types of improvements should be implemented throughout the Sprint as they are discovered, the Sprint Retrospective represents an opportunity to focus on both adaptation and inspection in a more formal and focused context.

Chapter 4: Artifacts of Scrum

A Scrum artifact is anything that represents work or value to provide transparency and opportunities for inspection and adaptation. Scrum artifacts are all designed specifically to maximize the transparency of relevant information to ensure that everyone has the same understanding of every aspect of the current Sprint or Increment.

Product backlog: The Product Backlog serves as an ordered list of everything that will ultimately go into the product. This document will be the sole source of requirements for any future changes that will be made to the product. The Product Owner will be the one who is ultimately responsible for the backlog of the product, including things like ordering, determining availability and generating content.

Regardless of how much work is put into the product backlog at the start of the project, it is still going to be a living document which means it will never be truly complete. In fact, the earliest portion of its development is important as it makes it clear what the most clearly defined requirements as well as those that are most important when it comes to getting a working product up and running. The product backlog then evolves from there along with the uses it will have and the environments it will be used in.

The product backlog should ultimately include all the fixes, enhancements, requirements, functions and features that the product will eventually have in future releases. Items in the backlog should all have clearly defined attributes including things like value, estimate and order. These items also frequently include a type of test description designed to determine when it can be considered finished and fully integrated into the next Increment.

As a program starts to get regular use and gains value with users and the marketplace as a whole it generates additional feedback and, as a result, the Product Backlog becomes much more well-defined and extensive. These requirements never stop changing, which is part of the reason it is important for the backlog to be considered a living document.

It doesn't matter how many different Scrum teams are working together on a product, they should all be working from the same product backlog. Refining the product backlog is the process of adding further detail and cost / benefit analysis estimates to existing product backlog items. This process requires the additional revision and review of the items that are already on the list and the Development Team is primarily in charge of determining when this process takes place. A good rule of thumb is that this should take up no more than 10 percent of the Development Team's time. The Product Owner can also update the backlog and any of its items at any time at their discretion.

As a general rule, the higher that an item is on the product backlog, the more well defined it is. This, in turn, leads to more accurate estimates thanks to the increased clarity provided by all the additional details. Backlog items that are going to be dealt with next should be so refined that they can be easily fit into the time-box of the next Sprint because they are so well-defined which means they will be considered ready for selection when it comes time to plan the next Sprint.

In these instances, the Development team is responsible for all of the estimates, thought the Product Owner is not without a degree of sway as well. The Product Owner, in this case, will help by making it clear what trade-offs are available and answering any questions the Development Team might have.

Tracking progress: Throughout each Sprint, the total amount of work remaining should be able to be easily summed up. The Product Owner is responsible for tracking the amount of progress that has been made towards the end goal and updating this progress report after each Sprint Review. The Product Owner then compares the amount of work remaining at previous Sprint Reviews with the current review to ensure that everything is still proceeding apace. The resulting determinations should then be shared with the entire team.

There are many different practices when it comes to forecasting progress, including things like cumulative flows, burn-ups and burn-downs. None of this can ultimately replace the raw importance of pure empiricism, however, especially in complicated environments when the outcome is far from guaranteed.

Sprint backlog: The Sprint backlog is the product backlog for a specific Sprint as well as a place for delivering the requirements within the scope of the next Sprint. It can also be thought of as a forecast for the Development Team to all them to start considering what will need to be done in order to deliver the next Increment as effectively as possible.

The Sprint backlog is effective because it can make visible all of the work the Development Team considers necessary when it comes to meeting the current Sprint goal. To keep the continuous improvement rolling in, it should also include at least one major improvement as defined by the most recent Sprint Retrospective meeting. The Sprint backlog should contain enough details to make any changes that are made to it easily describable during the Daily Scrum.

When new work is required, the development team can add to the Sprint backlog directly. When the work is completed, the estimate for any remaining work should be updated as well. If specific elements of the plan are ultimately cut for one reason or another, they can then be easily removed. The Development Team is solely responsible for changing the Sprint backlog during the Sprint. As such, it serves as a real-time, extremely accurate, picture of the work the Team is currently working on and will finish by the time the Sprint is completed.

Tracking the progress of the Sprint: The total work that is left to do in the Sprint should be tracked in real time and summed up in a form that is easily accessible to anyone in the team. The Development Team should be in charge of tracking this work total, and updating it with each Daily Scrum to ensure the entire Scrum team knows the odds that the current goal is going to be achieved within the current Sprint.

Increment: The Increment can be thought of as the Product of all the added value the backlog items that have been completed during the Sprint have generated added to the value of all of the previous Sprints thus far. An increment can be thought of as a body of inspectable, completed work that supports the Sprint Goal as well as the end product goal that the Scrum Team is working towards.

Chapter 5: Scrum Master as Servant Leader

Responsibilities of a Servant-Leader

A ScrumMaster is a servant-leader in that it is their goal to facilitate the needs of all of the members of the team as well as anyone the team serves, which is typically the customer. They should strive to achieve results that line up with the goals of the Scrum Team as well as the larger organization's business objectives, principles and values.

ScrumMaster responsibilities may include:

- Setting up a Scrum framework in the service of the team, not as a way to command or micro-manage.
- Giving the Development Team the tools they need to manage themselves successfully.
- Mitigating conflict by ensuring that any disagreement is seen as a healthy exchange of ideas.
- Ensuring that every member of the team is fully versed in the ins and outs of the Scrum framework.
- Stepping in to handle anything that will get in the way of

the Scrum Team reaching the goals of their current Sprint.
- Doing anything that is required to remove any roadblocks that may come up during a Sprint.
- Ensuring everyone on all sides of the team are being as transparent as possible.
- Helping in any way possible that will lead to the team becoming better versions of themselves.
- Nurturing a collaborative, supportive and empathic culture within the team.
- Constantly keeping the team challenged and away from mediocrity.
- Ensuring development, growth, and happiness of team members.

The Scrum Master is a servant-leader for the Scrum team. To encourage Servant Leadership behavior, the Scrum Master role by design does not have organizational authority or power. The Scrum Master is not a boss or an alternate title for a manager of the team.

The absence of organizational power, allows the Scrum Master to establish Psychological safety within the team. This, in turn, empowers the team members and allows them to self-organize. If the Scrum Master possesses organizational power, that limits the chances of establishing a safe environment.

A Servant-leader Scrum Master creates an environment where people can contribute and flourish. An environment where people are cared for and feel safe to express themselves. An environment where they've enough empowerment to make necessary decisions. Scrum Master is that leader for the Scrum team.

Who does the Scrum Master serve? The Scrum Master serves the Development Team, the Product Owner, and the Organization in their endeavor to apply Scrum and get benefits from it.

A Scrum Master enables the Scrum Team to become a high performing team. So much so, that it can rapidly adapt to the changing customer needs and solve customer challenges. For those Scrum Masters who also happens to have organizational authority - aka responsibility of product delivery, the team members reporting into you, you make financial decisions, you write performance reviews, etc. observe your behavior closely.

A good servant-leader Scrum Master should be able to answer the following questions:

If asked, will my colleagues and team members say that I serve them?

Whose agenda do I serve? Theirs or mine?

Am I able to justify the responsibility as a Servant-Leader Scrum Master?

How does Scrum Master's Servant-Leadership style work with traditional managers? The paradoxical style of Servant Leadership is difficult to enact for the traditional managers. Most managers tend to be comfortable with the leadership aspect, but not the servant aspect.

Servanthood and Caring: As a Scrum Master, you do not have any authority in the organization. You derive influence from your subject matter expertise of Scrum and by having the heart to serve your team and care for them.

As a Servant-Leader, you seek to empower the team members and invite them in decision making. Your behavior is of serving and caring. It enhances the growth of team members while improving the caring and quality of organizational life.

Is your emphasis on serving your team-members for their good and not just the good of the organization? If yes, then you sure are one effective Scrum Master.

Empowering and Helping: The Scrum Master needs to be concerned about what is going on with all of their stakeholders. Broadly stakeholders include society, communities, business partners and employees, and specifically the least privileged among them. Servant-Leader Scrum Masters believe that team members have an intrinsic value beyond their apparent responsibilities as employees. These Scrum Masters are deeply committed to the development and growth of each and every Scrum Team member. During their time spent as a Scrum Master, individuals need to learn to nurture the professional as well as the personal growth of team members.

Serving Team's Agenda: A Scrum Master as a servant-leader uses his capabilities and skills to help the team establish their agenda. The Scrum Master serves the team's agenda, not their own.

The Scrum Master does not impose any directions or mandate upon the team. A Servant-leader Scrum Master instead, believes in Change by Invitation. They invite the team to choose the goals and the direction. They invite team members to opt into, participate and keep options open for anyone to opt out.

It is important to understand that if a person is titled as a Scrum Master but also carries the traditional manager's responsibility to deliver a release or to manage the team members etc. They'll not be able to truly serve the team's agenda. Such a person will almost always end up making others follow their direction and agenda that they set.

There is also a boundary to serving team's agenda. For example: if a product owner's agenda is to finish a certain number of features by this sprint, however, the team clearly sees that as not practical. Though you want the Product Owner to succeed, however, in such situation it is your responsibility to shield the Development Team from the excessive pressure of the Product Owner. Often Scrum Masters give-in to the pressure and allow the PO to overload the Dev Team.

What do you think is the result in situations when the Development Team was asked to deliver more than they could practically deliver?

a) A product having defects and poor quality

b) Stressed and overworked Team members from having to work extra nights and weekends

c) Accrual of Technical Debt

In any of the situation, can you say the Team's Agenda was served?

Building Relationships: Establishing and nurturing long-term relationships with all stakeholders and keeping the team-members in focus helps them meet their fullest potential. If you are genuinely serving, caring and helping your team members grow, building relations with them will not be an issue. To build longer term relations, you would need to forgo short term approach/gains and allow for the things to settle.

Healthy relations with the team create a synergy among the team-members and boosts the team's performance and growth. Is your emphasis on building long term and healthy relationships? If yes, you are on track.

Being Humble: Like a good leader, the Scrum Master stays humble and practices regular self-reflection. Counter to a traditional leader's pride, servant leaders exhibit humility in their behavior. Servant leaders don't think less of themselves they just think of themselves less.

They have high self-confidence but very low situational confidence. If they are faced with a situation, their response would most likely be: I have the intellect to solve all the problems, but I don't have all the answers and for that, I need other people's brain.

In today's world where there are so much information and so

many tools, it's important to acknowledge that one person cannot know everything and that everyone needs or at some time will need his/her team members' help. A servant-leader will not take pride in the moments of success but will surely accept errors in times of failure.

Emotional Healing: Your people are going through change all the time. There is uncertainty and failures. Some of your people may have bruises. Many of them may go through emotional turbulences. Are you able to emotionally heal them? Offer your support?

As per the team development model, the team goes through Forming, Norming, Storming and Performing phases. While your team is going through Forming, Norming and Storming phase of the team development, as a Scrum Master, are standing by your team during this time of change? As a Servant-Leader, any emotional healing and support that you offer can go long way in building an environment of trust and care within the team.

Being Empathic: Being Empathic involves deeply connecting with the emotions of the other individual without judgement and critique. It is an essential behavior of Servant-Leaders. Empathy starts with listening. Genuinely being present at the moment with somebody and listening with your whole self helps to understand the other person's situation. Here the aim is to slow down and listen with the intent to understand the meaning behind the words, the meaning of what is being felt, and what is not being said. Empathy connects two people by heart. Connecting with someone by heart is much more powerful than connecting only through the brain.

For Scrum Masters who are not naturally empathic (count me in with you), being aware of and caring about others' emotions is the starting point of developing empathy. Empathically listening to what your team members say and acknowledging what you sense + hear.

Such as:

Elena, you seem to be worried. How can I help?

David, I hear you are concerned about Matt's behavior. What would you like to happen?

When you lend someone your empathic ears, they get it. They feel safe and comfortable to share even more. Scrum Master through Empathy builds relationships, heals the team members, earns trust and gains influence.

Being Ethical: The moral component of the Scrum Masters must be strong. Being ethical relates to the way in which a servant-leader makes choices, disciplines himself or herself and chooses the right thing to do in the service of the team. The Scrum Master may also encourage the team to self-reflect and establish high standards of moral and ethical behavior.

The team members constantly observe the moral basis of the servant-leader's actions and organizational goals and relate to them. If you as a Scrum Master have ingrained integrity and professionalism in yourself, it'll be possible to bring it to the team.

Often times, the Scrum Master may realize that the team needs to mature and they must be empowered, educated to handle their own meetings, hold each other accountable, collaborate with users and PO and deliver value. And if the time comes when the Scrum Master may not be providing the best value for the team and hence should decide to either step down from that role or move on.

Chapter 6: Making the Scrum Transition

While there are any number of reasons, that have already been discussed, that could be the turning point when it comes to your decision to transition your team to the Scrum framework, it is important to keep in mind that it's not without its share of difficulties as well. This chapter will look at many of the most common difficulties often associated with the transition and discuss the easiest ways to avoid them.

Team members resisting change: When it comes to the challenges that are often going to be faced when making a Scrum transition, perhaps the most frustrating for a future Scrum master is the covert, overt, passive and active resistance that you will likely face from the team. While the best way to deal with this resistance is likely going to vary from team to team, it is important to know what to look for so you can nip it in the bud as quickly as possible.

For starters, active resistance is the easiest to spot as it is often limited to a handful of jaded and grumpy individuals who don't like anything that gets in the way of how they do things. However, if this issue is not dealt with on a one on one, personal, level then these agitators could generate a galvanizing message that could spread to other team members until there is an active block to prevent the change from moving forward.

This will generally go hand in hand with overt resistance in which those who are against the change are actively bad mouthing the process and trying to talk even more team members out of participating. About the only good thing when it comes to overt resistance is the fact that it is easy to determine who is doing what so that you can get to the root of the problem as well. When you do deal with these individuals it is important to do it in such a way that you turn foes into friends as opposed to doing something that could further damage morale.

Unfortunately, overt resistance is not nearly as common as passive resistance which is far more difficult to pin down, and far more harmful to the cause as a result. While they may learn what to do, they will only ever do the bare amount of testing that they really need to do in order to get by without embracing the process to the extent that the process as a whole is likely to actually improve. This then leads to an even greater issue as it can mean errors aren't caught and other team members have to waste time covering for the person who resists.

Perhaps the most challenging part of dealing with resistance, however, is that it might be a subconscious response that occurs in a team member who appears to have completely bought into the process at first glance. Remember, just because a team member might know that Scrum is the right thing to do doesn't mean that it is the easiest thing to do, which is where the mental disconnect might come into play.

In order to break through this mental disconnect, the goal should be to create the sort of feeling within the organization that this type of change is inevitable. If team members understand that Scrum is already a done deal then they will be more likely to spend time fighting it and more time learning how to make the change as easy to handle as possible.

Motivation is another key factor in this instance as it is important to create a sense of urgency in the transition as well. Selling Scrum as a way of helping the company which is struggling, whether this is actually the case or not, can be an effective means of quelling doubt very quickly.

Misunderstanding of the process: As the Scrum process is so very different from many of its alternatives, it is extremely easy for team members to become confused, despite their best intentions. In fact, it is quite common for team members to assume they understand Scrum only to find out that they are actually mixing up a host of different, similar, processes.

In order to help get them in the right mindset, the first thing the team needs to understand is that what is occurring amounts to a true culture change for the company that will alter how every member of the team spends at least a portion of their day. One of the most common misunderstandings that are sure to arise is the idea of deadlines as opposed to estimates, which are very different things and can take some getting used to. It is important to keep in mind that true reeducation involves learning to think of production as a process which means learning to think in increments and manage expectations differently as a result.

Meetings: Depending on how the workplace was previously broken down, getting used to the idea of a cross-functional team where everyone understands the project can be quite a lot to swallow. If a strict policy on meetings isn't implemented early then you will find that people still attend far too many meetings each day and the team's productivity suffers as a result.

In order to properly address these issues, it is important that the team does a full transition to Scrum all at once as trying to go slowly will only further complicate the issue. At the same time, however, it is important to understand that the team will likely need some time to get comfortable with the lack of control from the top down and you will need to provide support during this time as well.

Intimidation factor: When teams start managing their own work, it means that each member will naturally have much more responsibility when it comes to decision making, prioritizing and scheduling which can feel like a lot of extra pressure. To counteract this fear, you need to make it clear that nearly all of these decisions are going to be made by the team as a whole. Another way to make this part of the process seem more manageable is to start with smaller teams right off the bat. This will keep the individual number of moving pieces quite low which, will, in turn, make the entire process seem less intimidating right from the start. If you have a larger team and you are starting off with smaller teams to make the process more manageable then it is important to also ensure that they always remain as cross-functional as possible.

Chapter 7: Tips for Success

Make a Point of Not Planning Up Front: Many teams, especially when they are first getting started with Scrum, still feel the need to do some type of planning before they get started. This can, in turn, lead to what is known as analysis paralysis. This occurs when the planning stage of any given project will often grind progress on that goal to a halt as buy-in is obtained from several different sources over the course of days, or even weeks. Don't forget, Scrum was designed to be an adaptable framework for inspection, which means that by its very nature it is antithetical to have several team members sitting around waiting for a single individual to finish preparing so they can get to work.

It is important to remember that in order for Scrum to be used correctly, users need to value the act of creation and, as such, the potential for failure inherent therein, not just the documentation of the process. It also values the individual bonds that ensure individuals work well together as opposed to blindly following a set group of rules. This means that while there is no harm in a certain individual from doing some early legwork on a project before bringing in the whole team, the point that this starts to be a detriment is where waiting for this one person starts keeping a larger number of individuals from generating any real type of value for a prolonged period of time.

While finding the right mixture of pre-production and production can be difficult at first as you don't have a clear idea of what exactly it is you are looking for from your team, it will get easier to pick out with practice. A good rule of thumb is that if it takes you more than two days to fully prepare for the start of a new project, then your team might be suffering from analysis paralysis.

Rather than taking the time to plan everything out up front, teams can instead simply get started and use the opportunities to provide feedback that is presented in the time allotted for Sprint Review to adjust workflow as needed. This can be even extended to the creation of the Product Backlog. What's more, things could even go so far as for the Product Owner to emerge empirically from the available stock of stakeholders instead of being arbitrarily assigned.

While you and your team may initially find that starting a sprint without first completing a product backlog can be difficult, it is nevertheless, completely possible assuming of course that the team already has at least a general idea of what is required in the business in question and a project or project charter to work from. Using this information, your team should be able to, at the very least, come up with a realistic idea of what their first Sprint should consist of prior to getting started. Remember, the key words here are getting started. The goal during this initial Sprint is to be able to come up with something that can be demoed, and possible even shipped.

While sometimes this will result in things that are completely wrong or otherwise not shippable, the point isn't to get everything right straight out of the gate but to instead get everyone working through the Inspect and Adapt cycle as quickly as they can. This, in turn, will require actual stakeholders to attend the demo at the end of the initial Sprint in order for you to determine how successful it actually is.

Don't Worry About Advanced Tools: It is common for new teams to put off starting the Sprint process while they look through the myriad of different types of tools that are available to help them make using Scrum as simple and easy as possible. While there is nothing wrong with looking into finding a good Scrum assistance tool, it is important to wait to do so until you have a clear idea of just what facets of the Scrum process that you need electronic help with.

The impetus to do so is obvious, especially in teams that already work for technology companies. After all, why wouldn't you use technology to solve this problem as well as all of your others? In reality, however, Scrum electronic tools can often be more difficult to work with then their more analog equivalents. This occurs for several different reasons that can generally be broken into three different categories. First, they actually make it more difficult to freely share knowledge. Second, they actually can make the information that is shared through them successfully less clear while at the same time they make the information that is shared available more slowly to interested parties.

Looking into fancy tools this early in the process is akin to putting the cart before the horse, it is more important to get started at all then to get started in the perfect way with the perfect tools. Being extremely particular about a specific tool set is an easy way to put off starting to use the Scrum system while still feeling productive about doing so. Don't let yourself fall into this trap, get started with what you have available and work on improving from there.

When first getting started using the Scrum system, you should find that all of your tracking needs are easily met with a simple pen and paper tracking system. This will let you get started quickly and easily and get into your first Sprint without first ensuring that everything is as absolutely perfect as possible. Additionally, most of the time you will find that the simplest and most effective way of reliably improving communication within your team is by simply ensuring that everyone who is working on a given project is physically located near one another.

Additionally, you are going to want to ensure that the space has plenty of whiteboards or other writing spaces and that everyone is facing the center as opposed to being segregated off into their own little spaces. Finally, you are going to want to ensure that the group is separated from the rest of the organization so they feel as though they have a bit of privacy.

Keep your Product Owner Involved: A common problem that many Sprints face over time is a Product Owner who is energized and eager to contribute at the start of the Sprint, but who then falls off when the time comes to actually turn ideas into reality. A Product Owner is just as much a part of a Sprint team as anyone else which means they should ideally be present at every Daily Scrum as well as during the Sprint Planning Meeting and the eventual Sprint Retrospective and Review. The Product Owner will also need to be available during work hours to provide input as needed to team members with questions. Essentially, when the Product Owner is not actively dealing with shareholders they should be involved in the Sprint Process.

Remember, the Scrum Team model was created with the express purpose of being as beneficial to productivity, creativity and flexibility as possible, but it can only do this when the Product Owner is as committed to respect, openness, focus, courage and commitment as the rest of the team. The only exception to this is if your team follows the strictest, most recent interpretation of Scrum which limits the Daily Scrum to the development team exclusively. There is still the option for others to observe the meeting, however, and this should include both the Product Owner as well as the Scrum Master.

While early on in your team's experience with the Sprint, it may be difficult to determine if your Product Owner is putting in enough time and effort, you will be able to tell if they added enough input, however, by how they respond to your Sprint Review. If during the Review, the Product Owner uses the time to provide feedback on the results then you will know they weren't involved in the process enough. The sign of an involved Product Owner is when they are leading the discussion with stakeholders, users or customers during the Sprint Review instead.

While the Product Owner needs to be as available as possible, there are numerous different scenarios where they may need to legitimately be absent from the process for a prolonged period of time. First and foremost, is when they are working with shareholders, though these types of meetings should be scheduled separately from Sprint based commitments in most cases. Regardless, it is going to be best for the Product Owner to leave a surrogate in place to provide their input for them based on the information that is already readily available.

Don't Use Stretch Goals: Stretch goals have long been used in many settings as a way of planning out additional goals that can be reached assuming certain conditions are met. They are antithetical to the Sprint methodology, however, and should never be used while on a Sprint for any reason.

There are two different types of stretch goals that can try and creep into your Sprints, it is important that you are aware of both of them and where they come from so that the Scrum Master can ensure they stay away from the positive team-centric attitude that the Sprint is cultivating. The worst type of stretch goal that can often appear to ruin group cohesiveness is the stretch goal that is suggested by someone from outside of the team.

Stretch goals that include a predetermined scope and deadline are the most difficult for Scrum teams to work through simply because it requires the team to start with a deadline and then work backwards to determine how to complete it, practically the opposite of how things normally go. What's worse, when objections are raised, they are typically met with either a reaffirmation to "get it done" or by simply adding more people to the team which does nothing to improve the state of things if the new individuals don't actually know anything about Scrum.

Otherwise, stretch goals have been known to pop up from time to time when members of the team try and determine what the Development Team is capable of, despite the Development Team's objections. It is important to keep in mind that the Development Team is going to have the best idea of what it can accomplish given various external limitations and wasting time disagreeing with them is, quite simply, time that can be better spent elsewhere.

The solution to this common issue is exceedingly simple, let the team determine the amount of work it can realistically get done within the confines of the Sprint. This doesn't mean that the first assessment of what is going to be done is going to be set in stone, but it does mean that no member of the team should ever feel pressured to commit to more work than they feel they can realistically complete. Forcing a team to commit to stretch goals is likely to build distrust among team members if the stretch goals are not met successfully. Distrust can lead to resentment and both will ultimately result in lower quality work being produced time and again. After all, if the stretch goal failed then there must ultimately be a reason why do your team a favor and avoid stretch goals and the witch hunts that they will always ultimately engender.

Make it Clear that Individual Sacrifice is Not Required: When your team is in the middle of a Sprint, they are going to routinely be forced to work through complex problems on the fly. There is a right way and a wrong way to solve these problems, however, and the lines regarding which is which can seem blurry without the right context. First and foremost, it is important to understand that the team naturally improves by coming together and solving these sorts of problems, which not only makes the unit as a whole more prepared for the future but more cohesive as a team as well. As such, if one person cracks the nut the entire team was working on then great, but if that person goes to near super human lengths to do so, then the team learns a very different lesson instead.

Rather than learning to work together to solve problems, the team in this case then learns to rely on the person who they know will always come through in a pinch. What's worse, this person could then start having an inordinate amount of pull over the team as a whole which means they could end up assigning mandates and even setting stretch goals without even realizing they are doing so. They can also cause several other types of issues for the team, starting with preventing the other members from developing an ability to creatively experiment and solve problems.

If one individual always has all of the answers then they are robbing others of learning why certain answers exist, which harms the team as a whole overall. If this proceeds unchecked for a prolonged period of time, then it is also likely that certain members of the team will become apathetic about the process as a whole because it will quickly become apparent that relying on the star is out of place with traditional Scrum practices. Ultimately this will break down the concept of the team at its base level and nothing will be accomplished, even if the star is still doing everything in their power to shine.

The easiest way to avoid this type of issue is to nip it in the bud during the planning for the Sprint. As long as things are planned properly from the beginning, there should be no need for any individuals to have to step up in any extreme way to get things done. Additionally, you may find it helpful to pad out your Sprint times if you find this type of scenario forming on a regular basis so that you can prevent things from devolving towards the need for such feats in the way they previously have before.

Chapter 8: Stories from the Trenches

Terminales Portuarios Peruanos: This is a company built around port and maritime services in Peru. Their IT group develops software for its own internal processes and operations. Traditionally it had worked along a predetermined release map that, increasingly, wasn't hitting the targets it needed to. With a team of 50 people, the goal was to deliver a new product at the end of each cycle but the process wasn't iterative and the teams were always held up at the end of development which made it difficult for them to meet their goals. IT group's ability to deliver new software every 30 days. The company chose to implement Scrum to scale by minimizing and removing cross-team dependencies and integration issues while elevating transparency.

In 2017 the company came up against a future deadline that it new it absolutely had to meet so it went about setting up a Scrum team to ensure the deadline was met without issue. Their initial phase of the implementation process started by bringing together stakeholders to align business objectives with user needs before aligning the results with the Product Backlog. The Product Owner also worked with the teams and used Impact Mapping and Story Mapping to help order and refine the Product Backlog. The Product Owner and the teams worked together to focus on creating integrated software.

The organization delivered products with a traditional project management model that prioritized schedule management and activity tracking to a model based on product delivery and daily progress. The first release was launched within one month and the product was in production completely by three months. The traditional model would have seen the first release within three months.

Vodafone: Vodafone, one of the largest mobile communication providers in the world, operates in more than 30 countries around the world and partners with outside providers of nearly 50 more. One of these partners, Vodafone Turkey, provides service to more than 20 million subscribers but the telecommunications industry in Turkey is extremely competitive and they needed help to manage the extreme Time to the Market pressure they were feeling.

Overall, there were three situations that needed to be dealt with in order for the pressure being put on the demand for improved productivity to decrease. The first was the time to market pressure, but there were also increased business expectations, an extremely long time-to-market period and a communication gap between all parts of the team. While the first issue could only be solved by improving the second and third, Scrum had answers for each.

The long period of time between when a product was developed and brought to market was due to the fact that testers and developers were considered to be separate units as opposed to one Development Team. As a result, the delay between the handoff for the two was significant and also decreased the responsiveness of IT as a whole. Likewise, the communication gap that the previous system created was solved by the added transparency that comes to the Scrum Framework and the understanding that everyone is working towards the same Sprint Goal at the same time.

To counter these issues the company set up a Scrum Team within the IT department in hopes of shortening their turnaround time while increasing the quality of the overall product as well. Under this pilot program, several Sprints were performed with this new Scrum team and the progress between each was tracked. Thanks to the added efficiency found in the Scrum framework, the pilot team ended up tripling its overall output in just three months.

Faced with such impressive results, the company decided to move forward with scaling the Scrum framework throughout the company. After about five months of getting things situated to the new way of doing things, the company reported that, across the board, the Scrum teams were performing at double the efficiency that was seen with the old model. What's more, the company also noted a marked decrease when it came to customer complaints as well as reported defects.

SoftwarePeople: All the way back in 2004, a company by the name of SoftwarePeople, based in Denmark, partnered with an investment firm in Bangladesh and made the decision to create a new subsidiary company in Bangladesh directly. Then, it hired 20 people in a single week and started using traditional processes in both offices with the end goal of receiving a CMMI level 3 certification in about 18 months. This led to nothing but countless pit stops and hurdles until the team switched back to Scrum in an effort to promote easier communication. The end result was the cessation of long-running projects, difficulties when it came to integration and technical issues and the adoption of smaller work batches, improved integration at all levels and a much faster delivery of clear business value.

It started in 2006 when the company was looking for a way to get away from their CMMI process that wasn't working. Someone within the company had heard about Scrum and everyone thought it sounded interesting so the CTO and three of the project managers decided to give it a shot and took a

Scrum Master training course. That same month the CEOs from both countries got together to receive Product Owner training in the UK to ensure they had a shared understanding of what made Scrum unique.

Soon after they started experimenting with Scrum in the Danish office when a particular complex project appeared on the horizon Not only was the Scrum team able to complete the project with flying colors, their results were so compelling that they convinced the company to institute a rollout of the framework to both offices.

Their implementation strategy revolved around starting with Scrum teams working on customer and research and development projects so that they could develop a reliable rhythm. The process would then expand to global teams who would now be able to work together more easily due to the additional understanding Scrum brought to the project. After a number of Sprints, they saw positive results across the board and a 100 percent increase in efficiency in some cases. While some team members still had questions from time to time, everyone generally had a much clearer idea of what their responsibilities were and what tools they had to ensure they met their goals.

Conclusion

Thanks for making it through to the end of *Scrum: The Complete Step-By-Step Guide to Managing Product Development Using Agile Framework*, let's hope it was informative and able to provide you with all of the tools you need to achieve your goals.

Just because you've finished this book doesn't mean there is nothing left to learn on the topic, and expanding your horizons is the only way to find the mastery you seek.

The Scrum framework offers something for virtually every type of business, but it is important to understand that it takes time to start seeing even the most basic of results. As such, if you are preparing to be the flagbearer for Scrum at your company it is important that you understand that it will be quite some time before you will start seeing results as getting a Scrum team to work together effectively is all about training and practice. Even with the short-term hit to productivity, however, the end result will still prove far more effective which is why it is still a quality value proposition despite the required training. Remember, molding your team into a Scrum team is a marathon, not a sprint, which means slow and steady wins the race.

Finally, if you found this book useful in anyway, a review on Amazon is always appreciated!

www.ingramcontent.com/pod-product-compliance
Lightning Source LLC
Chambersburg PA
CBHW071430220526
45469CB00004B/1478